Stars of Days & Months

The Story Of 7 and 12

Dedicated to star gazers. Even the darkest skies have lights for those who look.

© Copyright Mfg Application Konsulting Engrg (MAKE) 2012
All rights reserved. Teachers may copy this book for classroom use.
ISBN 978-1-933589-82-4
Front Cover picture is from NASA. Back cover is from Wikipedia and Pepe Robles

Table of Contents

Page	Description
1	Ancient Star Gazers
4	Sunday - Sun
6	Monday - Moon
8	Tuesday – Mars - Tiws
10	Wednesday – Mercury – Woden
12	Thursday – Jupiter – Thor
14	Friday – Venus - Frigga
16	Saturday – Saturn
18	Zodiac
20	January – Capricorn - Janis
22	February – Aquarius – Februa
24	March – Pisces – Mars
26	April – Aries - Aperire
28	May – Taurus - Maia
30	June – Gemini - Juno
32	July – Cancer – Julius Caesar
34	August – Leo – Augustus
36	September – Virgo - Septem
38	October – Libra – Octo
40	November – Scorpio – Novem
42	December – Sagittarius - Decem

A year is the time it takes the earth to travel once around the sun. Long ago, people looked up to the sky for how to divide the year.

Thousands of years ago, the Sumerians and Babylonians of the Middle East noticed the night sky. They saw stars that didn't move and five "stars" that did.

These ancient people created the 7 day week and the 12 month year. They believed the stars had power over people's lives. They gave days and months names based on the "stars" they could see.

Today, we know that these five moving "stars" are actually planets. We need to remember that people long ago watched the sky with only their eyes. Telescopes had not been invented.

They made up a 7 day week based on the 5 planets they could see and the sun and moon.

Seven day weeks and twelve month years based on star names spread west to Greece and Rome and east into Asia

Today, the weekday names in the Spanish, French, Chinese, Hindi and Thai languages still show the planet connection. Most of the names were changed in English.

Sunday

Sunday is named after the biggest circle in the sky, the sun. Without the sun, there would be no life on earth. Little wonder, the ancients worshiped the sun.

Wikipedia

NASA - Public Domain

5

Monday

Monday is named after the moon. The moon does not have its own light. It reflects sunlight. As the moon moves around the earth, the sun shines on it. This makes the different moon phases seen by us on earth. So moonbeams are really just bounced sunbeams.

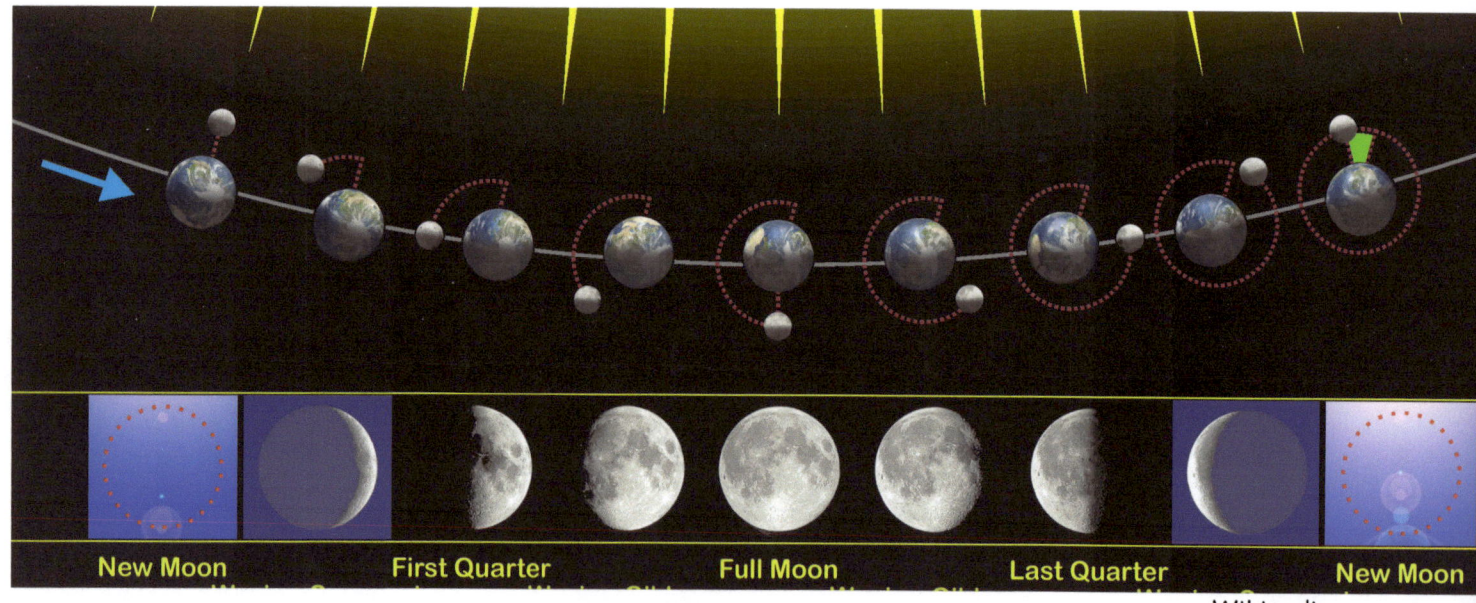

Tuesday

This day is named after the fourth planet from the Sun. The Romans called it Mars after their god of war. The English Tuesday is named after the Viking god of war, Tyr or Tiw.

Sometimes the planet Mars appears to be a blood-red color..

Wednesday

This day is named after the planet closest to the Sun. Romans named the planet, Mercury after their god of Trade. He is also the god who guides the dead to the afterlife.
The Saxon god, Woden is like Mercury. Wednesday is named after Woden.

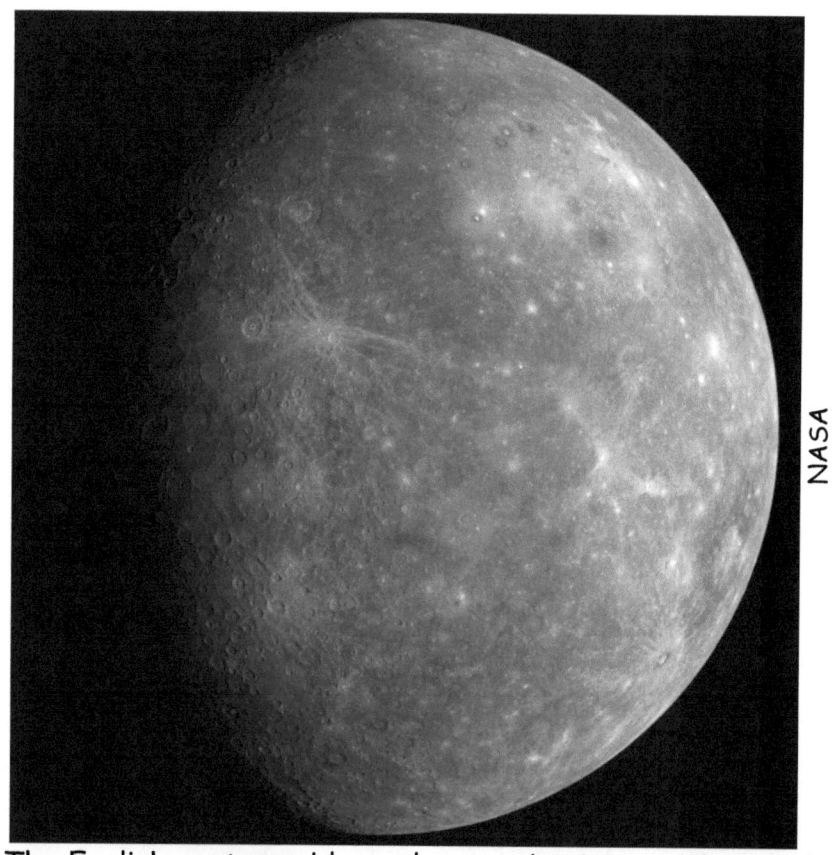

The planet Mercury is the fastest to orbit the sun.

The English root word 'merc' means business. The words merchandise and mercantile still show this connection.

Thursday

This is the biggest planet that circles our Sun. The Romans named this planet after their most powerful god named Jupiter. He was called Zeus by the Greeks.

The Vikings named this day after their god of thunder called Thor. So I wonder. If it thunders on Thursday is it just Thor celebrating his day?

NASA

Why did the English change weekday names away from the planets?
Could be because the sky in England is often too cloudy to see them.

Friday

The Romans named the brightest planet after their goddess of love and beauty. In English, Friday is named after the Viking goddess Frigga also called Freyja. She is Woden's wife. So when we say "thank god it is Friday", which god are we thanking?

Saturday

This day is named after the ringed planet. In Roman mythology, The god Saturn is Jupiter's father. Jupiter overthrew is father, Saturn, so Jupiter became king of the Roman gods. It gives new meaning to "taking over your father's business."

The English name for this day still shows the connection back to the planet Saturn.

Every day the earth spins around once. Every year the earth moves once around the sun. Because the earth is moving, different groups of stars are seen in the sky at different times of the year. The Babylonians connected groups of stars together to make 12 religiously significant signs called the Zodiac.

The number 12 comes from the fact that in a year, the moon goes through about 12 cycles from crescent to full. The Babylonians named the months after zodiac signs. Connecting stars into dot to dot shapes of the zodiac takes lots of imagination.

The Ancients didn't have electricity so they had lots of time to stare at the stars.

Wikipedia Ecliptic_path by Tau'olunga

January

At first, this month is called Capricorn, the sea-goat. This shows the importance of water and land to humans.

Romans named this month after Janus, the god of beginnings. Janus has two faces - one looks to the past and one looks forward to the future.

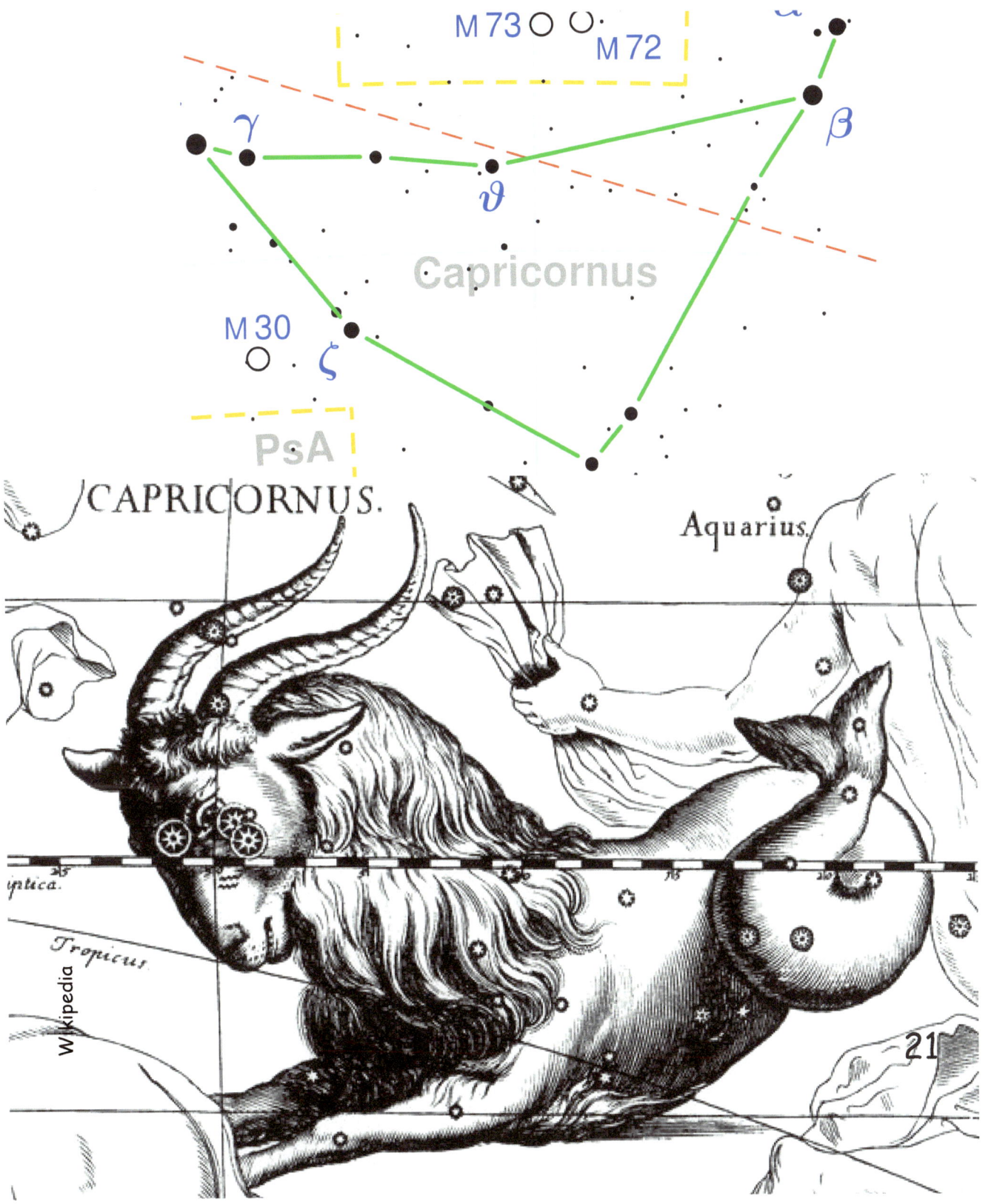

February

This month is named after Aquarius. He is possibly the god of rain and cleansing.

Romans named this month after the Februa Festival. Februa was a cleansing ritual. Everyone washed away their worries and renewed spiritually. Good idea to let go of problems.

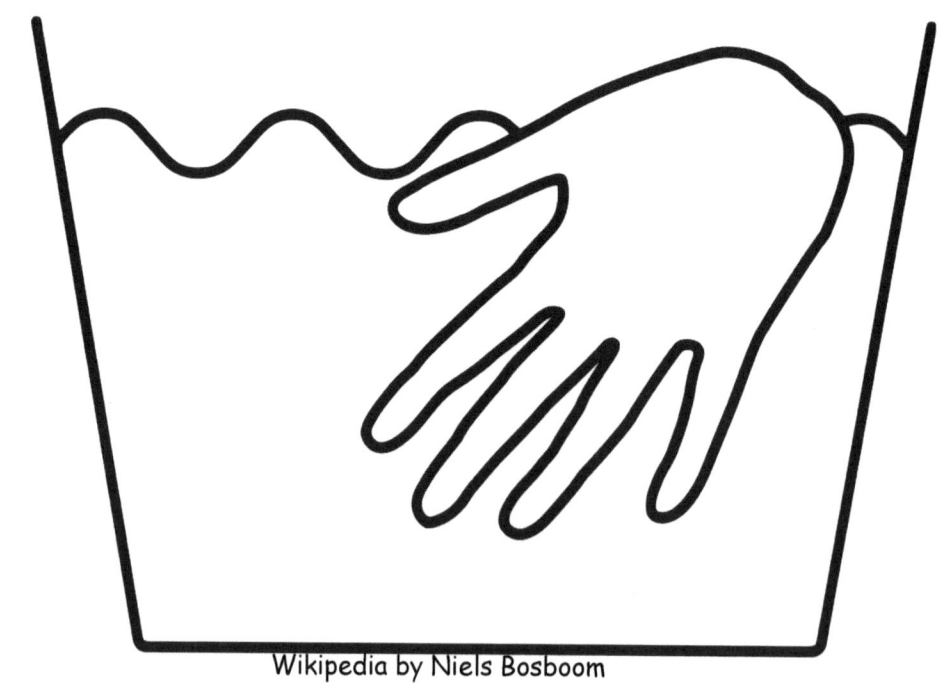

Wikipedia by Niels Bosboom

Wikipedia

March

The third month is named after the stars shape, Pisces the Fish. They are possibly a good luck sign for prosperity.

Romans changed the name of this month to honor their god of war, Mars. The Roman conquered all the countries around the Mediterranean Sea. They were often at war.

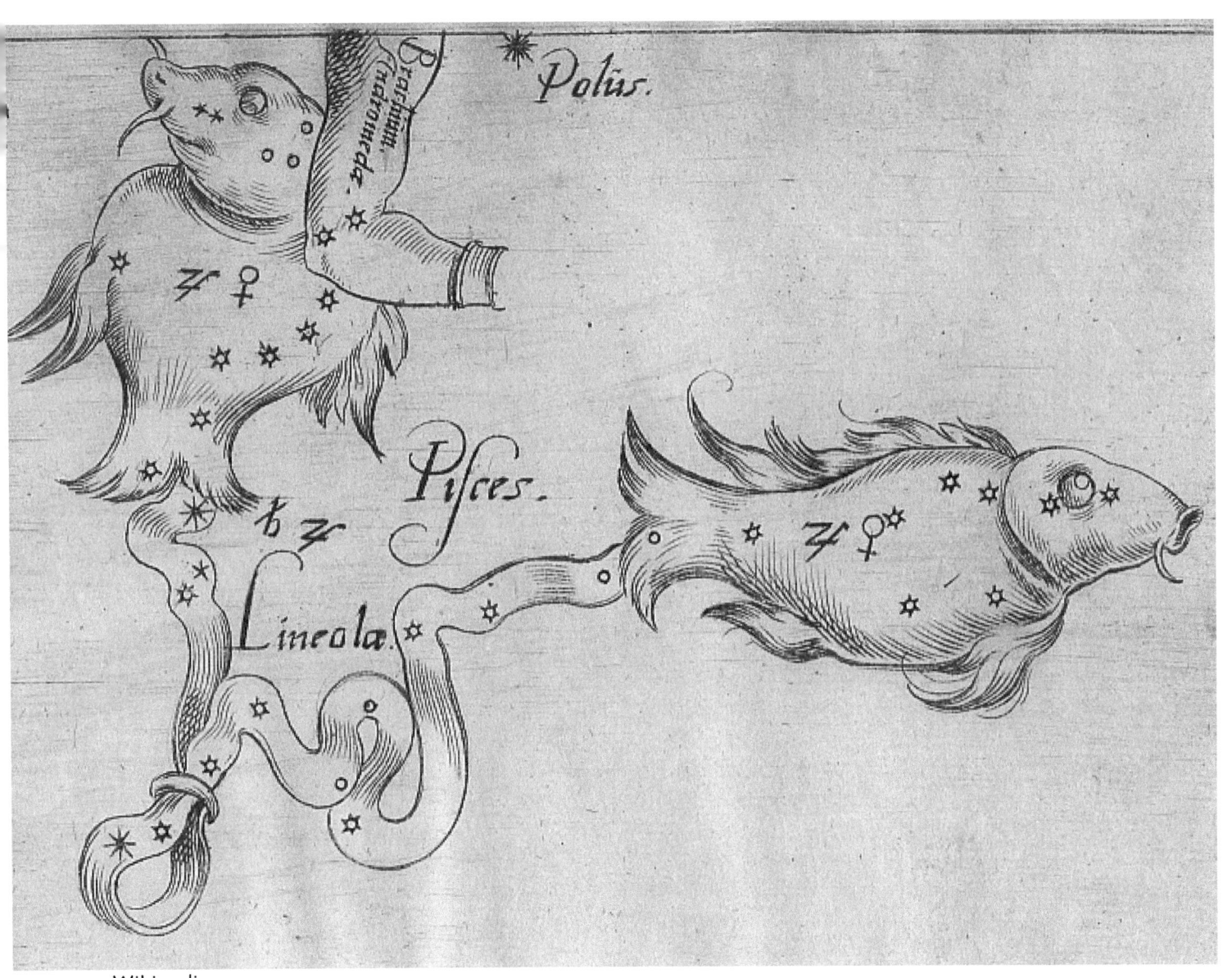

April

This month is named after Aries the Ram. Aries had golden hair, called a fleece. It is possible the ancients thought he was the source of gold. He may signify the search for fortune.

Romans changed the name to April which may come from the Latin word, Aperire which means "to open." April begins the Roman Springtime when plants open up.

27

May

This month is named after Taurus the Bull. People in the Middle East were the first to domesticate cows.

Romans named this month after Maia, their goddess of fertility and spring. In Rome, many crops bloom in May. Roman god Jupiter often came to earth as a bull avatar.

The goddess Maia is also the mother of the god Mercury. Jupiter is the father. Roman gods can be a bit naughty.

June

This month is named after the Gemini, Twins. The story is told, how one twin died. The caring gods turned the twins into stars that are always together. Romans named this month after Juno, queen of the gods. She is Jupiter's wife. In Western cultures, June is the most popular month to get married.

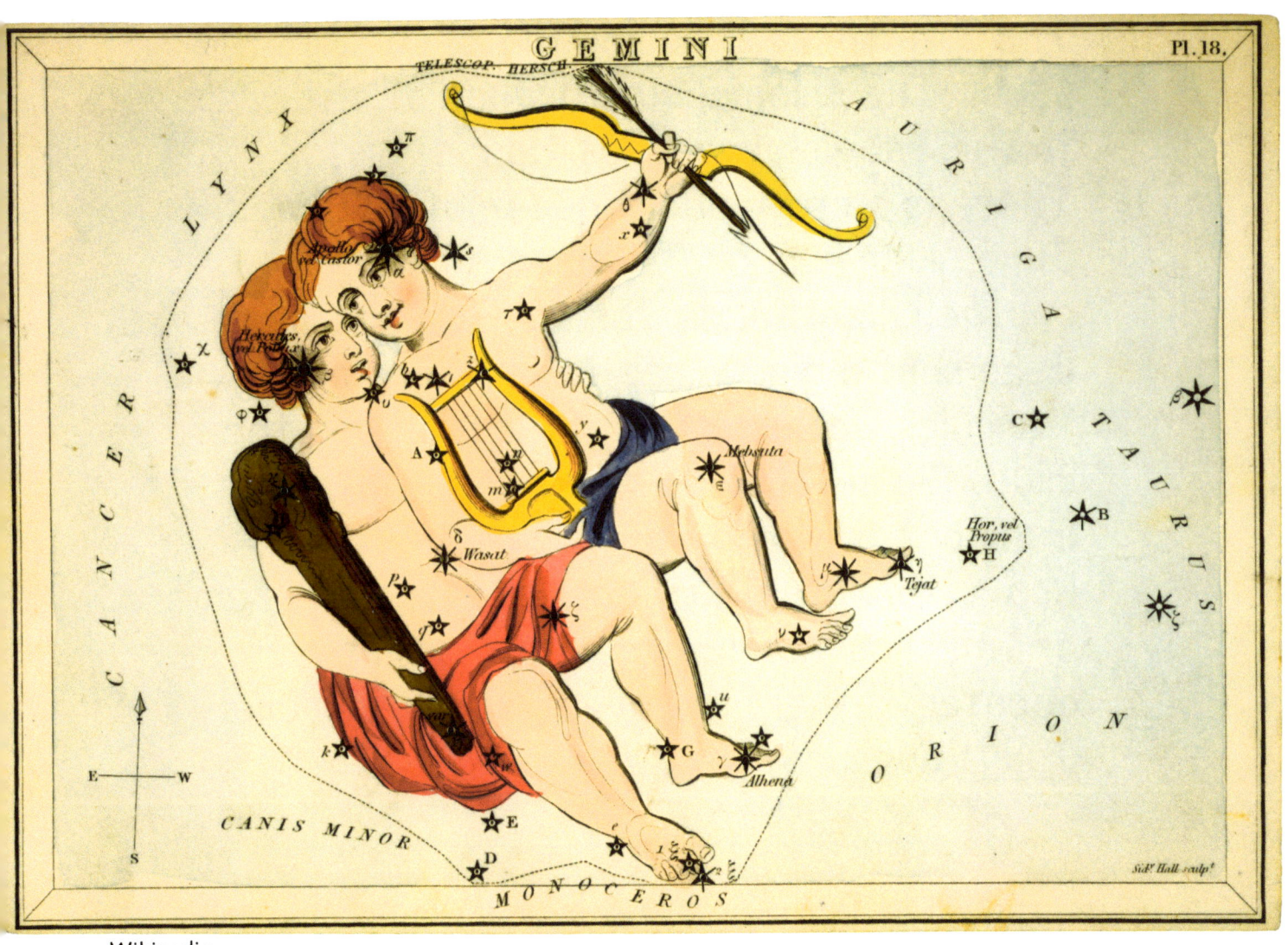

July

The 7th month is named after Cancer, the Crab. The original significance of the crab to the Babylonians is lost in history. There is a story about queen of the gods, Juno. Her husband Jupiter, fathered another illegitimate son named Hercules. Juno sent a giant crab to kill Hercules. Hercules was so strong that he killed the crab. To recognize the crab doing its duty, Juno put the crab into the sky as stars. Roman Emperor Augustus changed the name of this month. He named it after his adopted father, the great Roman General <u>Julius</u> Caesar.

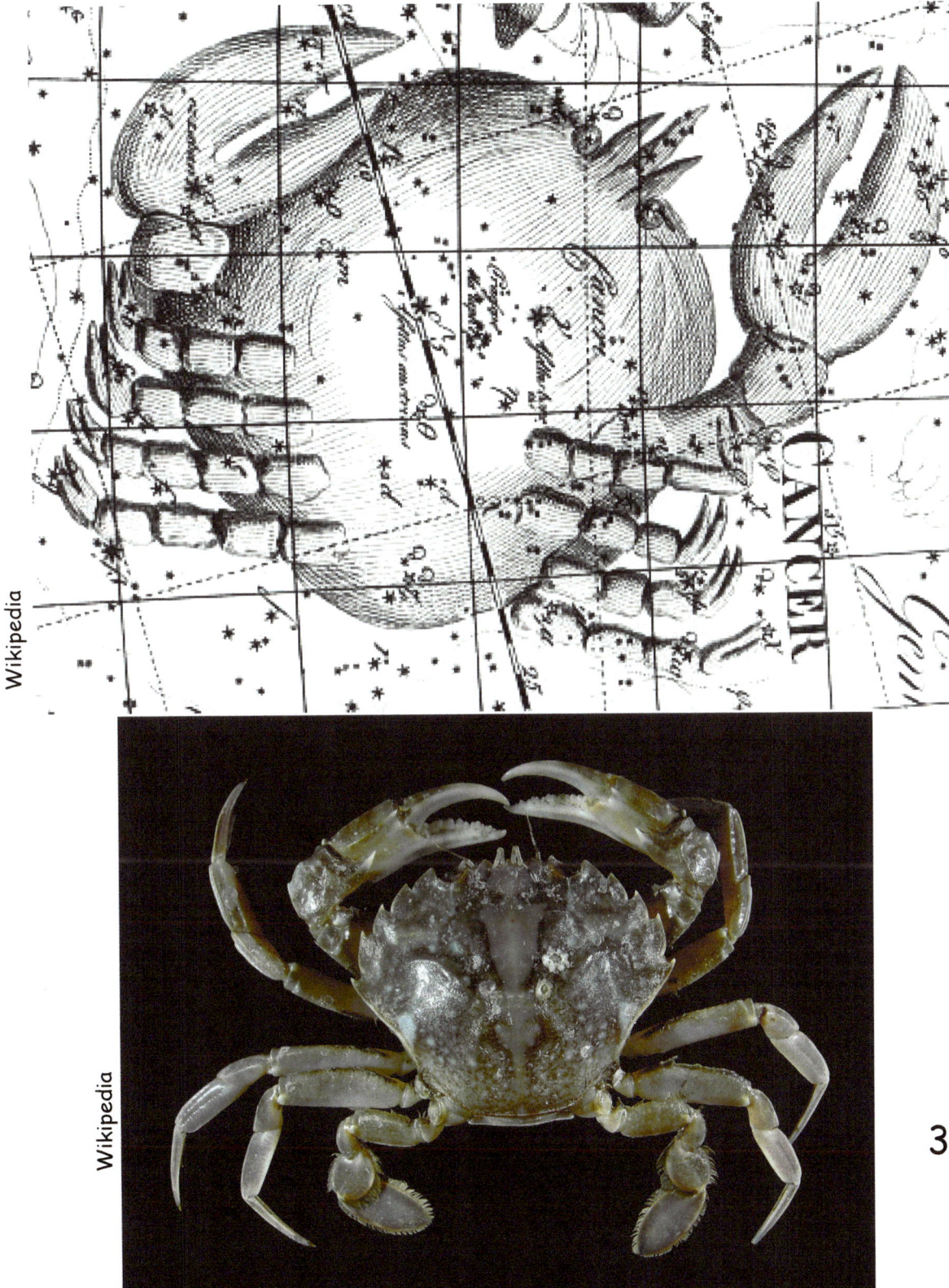

August

This month is named after Leo, the Lion. The lion is shown on the city walls of Babylon. The lion is a sign of courage. Roman Emperor Augustus, you know the guy who changed the name of July, also changed the name of this month. Who did he name it after? Himself of course.

Wikipedia

Wikipedia

35

September

The Babylonians named this month after Virgo, the Virgin. She represents innocence. The Greeks called her the goddess of justice. Ok, this is where it gets a little confusing.

Romans changed the name of this month to the Latin word, septem which means seven. The Romans didn't count the first two months.

How funny is that? The English word September, which is the name for the ninth month, comes from the Roman word for the number seven?

A heptagon is a seven sided shape.

Wikipedia

October

The Babylonians named the 10th month after Libra, the Balancing Scale. To them, it probably represented business and trade.

To the Greeks and Romans, Libra was the goddess of balance and truth.

Can you guess what the Romans named this month? They named it after their number eight, octo. Remember this is all because they didn't count the first two months of the year. I guess no one really likes cold winter months.

The word octagon, means an eight sided shape.

November

The 11th month is named after Scorpio, the Scorpion. There was once a great hunter named Orion. He boasted he could kill any animal. However, a scorpion named Scorpio stung Orion and he died. The Ancients believed that the gods put the scorpion in the sky to remind humans not to boast.

Can you guess what the Romans called this month? Yup! They named it after the Latin number nine, novem. Latin is the language that the Romans spoke.

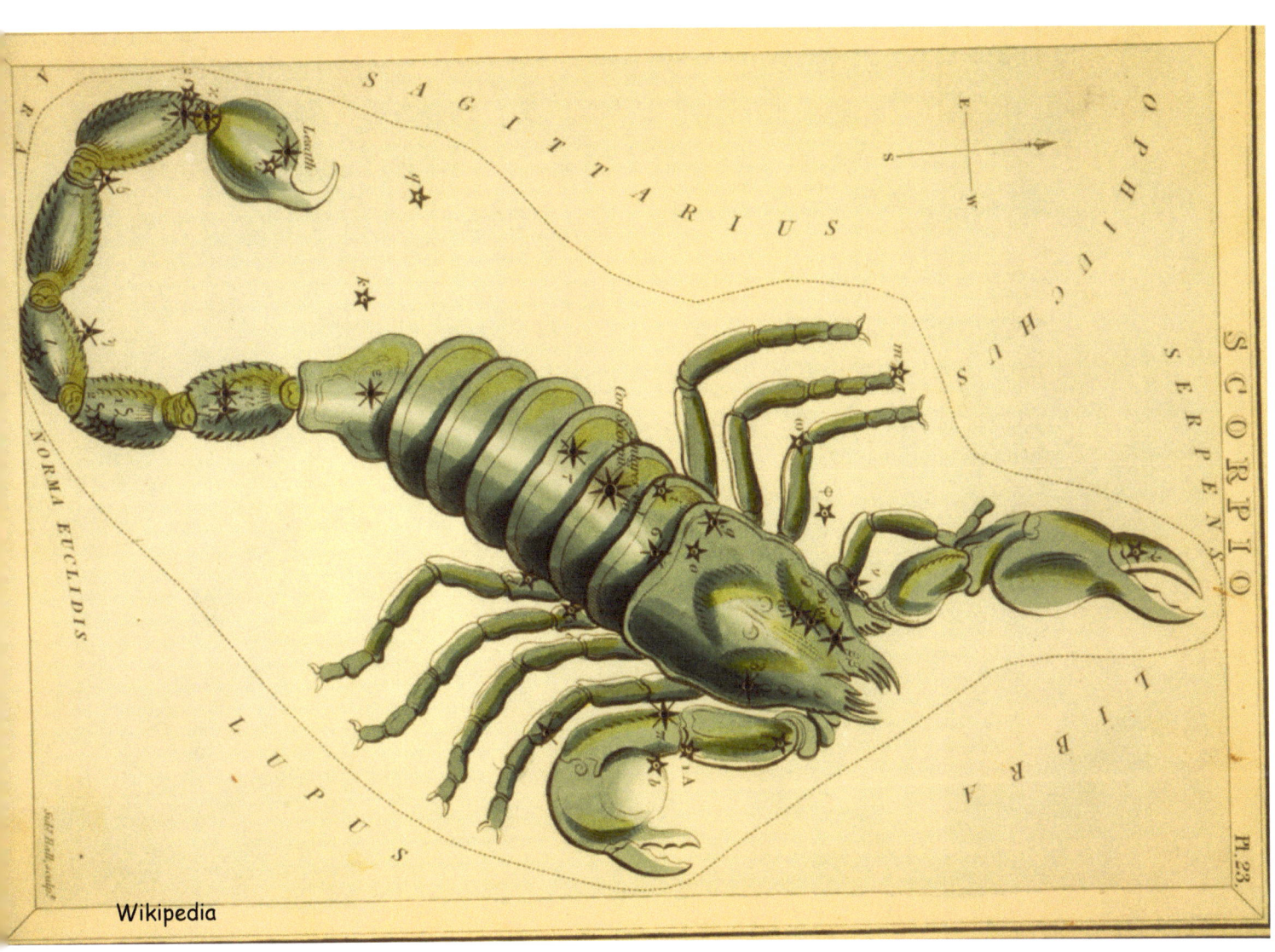

December

The 12th month is named after Sagittarius, the Archer. The Ancients believed the half-man, half-horse gave his life for another. To honor his compassion, the gods put him in the sky.

Romans named this month, no surprise, after the Latin word for 10, Decem. The word 'decimal' shows this connection too.

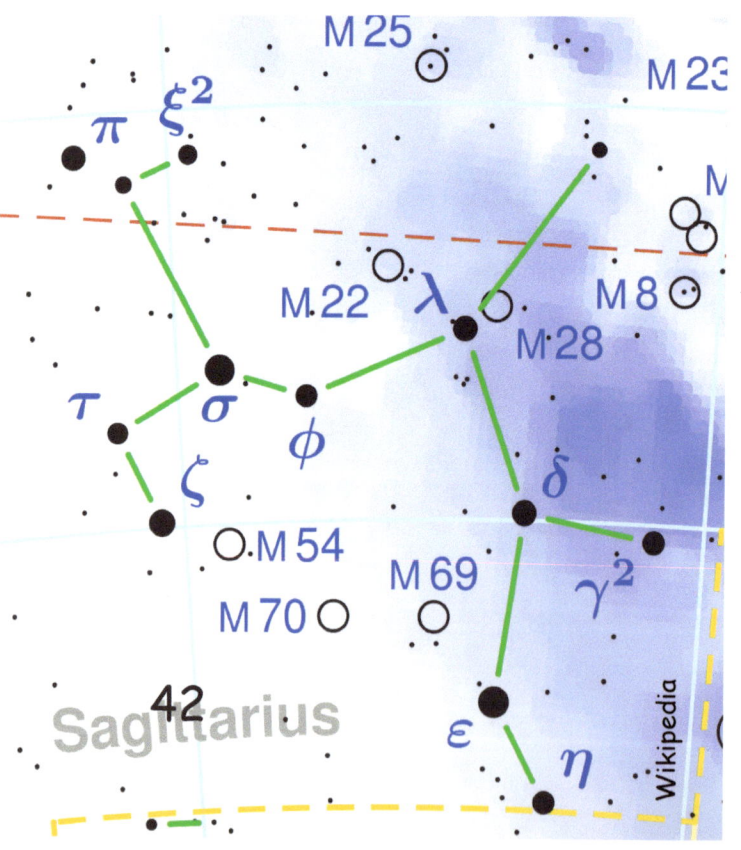

The numbers 7 and 12 were religiously important to Ancient people. The stars are still important to many today like those who follow astrology. Every time we tell time we are using "stars" that the ancients saw.

Everyone who appreciates the weekend, should be glad the world uses a seven day week and not the ten day week that the ancient Egyptians used. There are dozens of examples of the number twelve in modern life. Midyear, there are 12 light and 12 night hours in a day. There are sixty seconds in a minute and sixty minutes in an hour. Sixty is divisible by 12. The circle has 360 degrees for the same reason. There are 12 apostles. The Chinese calendar has twelve year cycles with animal names. Oh and by the way, there are 12 in a dozen.

Seven day weeks and twelve month years connect us through stars and time to those who lived before us. Now, that is something to thank our lucky stars for.

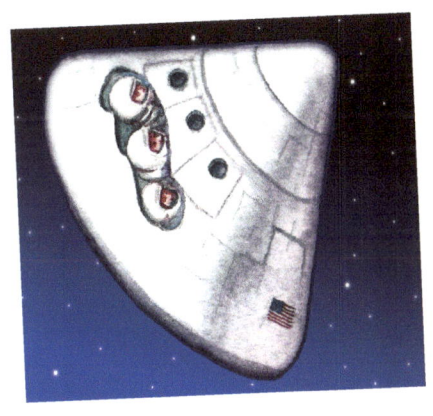  

Buy our other books at:

http://www.trythai-ketco.com

Our e-books educate and entertain

Sala Thai Restaurant in Goodyear AZ

- Home
- Loyalty Rewards
- Menu
- Take Out
- Current Specials
- Contact Us

432 North Litchfield Road • Suite 304
Goodyear, Arizona 85338
½ mile south of I-10

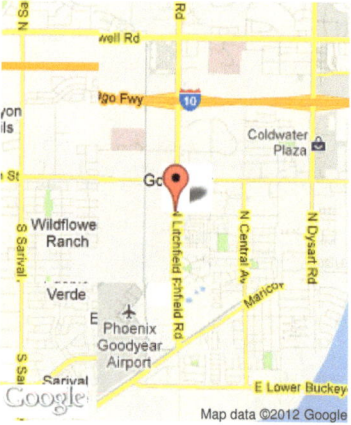

http://trythai-ketco.com

All Are Equal – From Slavery to Civil Rights
Brit Mu Briefly - From Seeds to Civilization
Catch Phrase Come-Froms - Origins of Idioms
Chase to Space – The Space Race Story
Civil Sense – What if There Wasn't a Civil War?
Common Come-Froms – Origins of Objects
Computer Come-Froms –To Count, Compute & Connect
Computer Patterns – A Ditty on Digital
Cozy Clozy – From Fibers to Fabrics
Essence of America – The I's in US
Essence of Science – 7 Eye Opening Ideas
Fishi and Birdy - A Fable of Friends
G Chicken & 5 K's - The Thai Alphabet
Images in Action - Why Movies Move

Books are also available at http://www.lulu.com
Please contact us at: trythaiketco@gmail.com

Meaning of Money - The American Way
Nature's Links of Life
Ogs, Zogs and Useful Cogs – A Tale of Teamwork
Paintings With Insects, Eggs & Oils – An Intro to Art
Robin's First Flight – Wings of Courage
Skylings – An Intro to Airplanes
Stars of Days & Months – The Story of 7 and 12
Turtle Jumps - A Tale of Determination
Where Cookies Come-From - From Dough to Delicious
Who Did What in World History? Past Echoes in the Present
Why is California Interesting? – Dreams of Gold
Why is England Interesting? – Worldwide Words
Why is Thailand Interesting? – Source of the Smiles
Why is the USA Interesting? - The 50 State Quarters

Books are also available at http://www.lulu.com
Please contact us at: trythaiketco@gmail.com

Recommend further reading:

Chase to Space
The Space Race Story

Written by Douglas J.
and Pakaket Alford
Illustrated by Tina Bilbrey

Brit Mu Briefly

Douglas J. & Pakaket Alford

Fishi & Birdy
– A Fable of Friends

Written by Douglas J. and Pakaket Alford
Illustrated by Lilly and Viet Le

Turtle Jumps!

Written by Douglas J. & Pakaket Alford
Illustrated by Tami Ashby

www.ingramcontent.com/pod-product-compliance
Lightning Source LLC
Chambersburg PA
CBHW041547220426
43665CB00002B/52